Instant Sencha Touch

Build native applications with Sencha Touch easily and efficiently

Hiren J. Dave

PUBLISHING

BIRMINGHAM - MUMBAI

Instant Sencha Touch

First published: October 2013

Production Reference: 1241013

Published by Packt Publishing Ltd.
Livery Place
35 Livery Street
Birmingham B3 2PB, UK.

ISBN 978-1-78216-598-9

www.packtpub.com

Credits

Author

Hiren J. Dave

Acquisition Editor

Rebecca Youe

Commissioning Editor

Shaon Basu

Technical Editor

Amit Ramadas

Copy Editor

Alfida Paiva

Project Coordinator

Sherin Padayatty

Proofreader

Kelly Hutchinson

Production Coordinator

Alwin Roy

Cover Work

Alwin Roy

Cover Image

Aparna Bhagat

About the Author

Hiren J. Dave is a software engineer who graduated from Sardar Patel University. He has more than five years' experience in the enterprise software industry. He is currently working as a Technical Head in The Design Shop. Hiren is passionate about researching and learning new technologies. He is also passionate about mobile application development. His expertise lies in developing cross-platform and native mobile application development. He also shares his knowledge with the world through his blog, `http://davehiren.blogspot.in`.

I would like to thank my family and friends for their support and encouragement.

www.packtpub.com

Support files, eBooks, discount offers and more

You might want to visit www.packtpub.com for support files and downloads related to your book.

Did you know that Packt offers eBook versions of every book published, with PDF and ePub files available? You can upgrade to the eBook version at www.packtpub.com and as a print book customer, you are entitled to a discount on the eBook copy. Get in touch with us at service@packtpub.com for more details.

At www.packtpub.com, you can also read a collection of free technical articles, sign up for a range of free newsletters and receive exclusive discounts and offers on Packt books and eBooks.

packtlib.packtpub.com

Do you need instant solutions to your IT questions? PacktLib is Packt's online digital book library. Here, you can access, read and search across Packt's entire library of books.

Why Subscribe?

✦ Fully searchable across every book published by Packt

✦ Copy and paste, print and bookmark content

✦ On demand and accessible via web browser

Free Access for Packt account holders

If you have an account with Packt at www.packtpub.com, you can use this to access PacktLib today and view nine entirely free books. Simply use your login credentials for immediate access.

Table of Contents

Instant Sencha Touch

Welcome to *Instant Sencha Touch*. This book is a hands-on guide that provides you with all that you need to explore the Sencha Touch framework and start building high performance cross-platform mobile applications. The book contains the following sections:

So, what is Sencha Touch? is a quick introductory section on Sencha Touch for new users. It explains the Sencha Touch framework and some of its features. This will help you understand more about Sencha Touch.

Installation gives you step-by-step details for downloading Sencha Touch SDK, understanding the SDK, setting up the development environment, and installing some of the useful tools for development.

Quick start – building a Hello World application gives you further introduction to the most used components and features of Sencha Touch in real-time applications. It includes the necessary UI components and data packages.

Top 12 features you need to know about introduces you to the most amazing features of Sencha Touch, such as animation, adaptive layout, event handling, component queries, charts, and the MVC structure. It also introduces you to native deployment and creating custom themes.

People and places you should get to know gives you references to resources available on various social media to know more about Sencha Touch.

So, what is Sencha Touch?

Sencha Touch is a powerful JavaScript framework powered by HTML5 and CSS 3 web standards built for mobile web. Sencha Touch enables your web applications to replicate almost all native UI features. Nowadays, most of the mobile devices support HTML5 and CSS 3 web standards; that's why Sencha Touch is widely recognized as a cross-platform development framework. It's packed with features such as smoother scrolling, animation, adaptive layouts, native packaging, and offline support. It has a rich set of controls such as carousels, lists, forms, and tabs to replicate native UI features of most of the mobile devices available in the market. All the components are touch-optimized and support adaptive layout. Sencha Touch uses vector graphics, so it supports almost all the resolutions of various mobile devices without much tweaking, and with adaptive layout, it supports orientations such as landscape and portrait. Also, it can quickly respond to switching requests from landscape to portrait and vice versa. Sencha Touch also supports data storage. Sencha Touch applications work on almost all the mobile platforms such as Apple, Android, BlackBerry, and Windows.

It's not just a framework for developing web applications. With the support of native packaging, Sencha Touch can be used to develop native applications. There are a number of options for native packaging, such as Cordova (earlier PhoneGap) and Sencha Touch native wrapper. This means that one single Sencha Touch application can be deployed to more than one mobile platform. It drastically saves time and the efforts of any developer.

A Sencha Touch application as a web application

With the growing use of mobile devices, it's important that your web application supports mobile devices. As we mentioned earlier that most of the mobile browsers support HTML5 and CSS 3 standards, Sencha Touch is widely used as a framework for mobile web application development. Most mobile applications don't need much hardware support; that's the reason why Sencha Touch can be used as a cross-development platform. The Sencha Touch web application works just like any other web application. It can be hosted on some server and with the domain name it can be accessed in any mobile browser. There is no special requirement for the server when we use Sencha Touch, since it uses JavaScript, HTML5, and CSS 3. All the processing happens on the client side in the browser, and that's the reason why the Sencha Touch app can be used offline as well. With the support for HTML5 local storage, it can store and access local data in the browser as well. Sencha Touch supports all kinds of events and gestures such as touch start, touch end, tap, double-tap, swipe, and pinch. It can also respond to keyboard events of mobile devices. Sencha Touch also supports JSON, JSONP, XML, and Ajax requests with data packages. This enables a developer to bind data to the UI to make data-driven web applications. In short, Sencha Touch is a complete package for developing mobile web applications.

A Sencha Touch application as a native application

There are some drawbacks of web applications. It does not have much access to hardware. It cannot respond to some hardware events such as when a camera is started. Also, to view web applications you need to have an Internet connection on mobile devices, which sometimes may not be available. Web applications do not support features such as APN (Apple Push Notifications). Sometimes, consumers also prefer native applications instead of web applications. Native applications are much more stable than web applications, since they are directly running on top of device hardware. But that does not restrict Sencha Touch from being a development platform. With the support of some native wrappers, Sencha Touch apps can be deployed as native applications. One of the major native wrappers used is Cordova (earlier known as PhoneGap). It supports all the mobile platforms such as iOS, Android, Windows, BlackBerry, and Symbian. A major advantage of developing native applications using Sencha Touch is that a developer does not have to build separate applications for each platform. One single Sencha Touch application, once developed, can be deployed to various app stores such as Google Play Store and Apple App Store after converting it to a native application. A Sencha Touch application, once converted to a native application, can communicate with hardware and use its features. Another reason to go for a native application is that it's more secure than web applications.

PhoneGap build is one of the nice tools used to convert Sencha Touch apps to native apps. It is accessible from `http://build.phonegap.com`. Here, we can upload our Sencha Touch applications and trigger the build for various platforms. Within few minutes, you will have deployable native applications for selected platforms.

Sencha Touch 2 has its own native wrapper, which can be used to package applications for iOS and Android. It also has HTML5 device APIs to communicate with hardware. It has improved performance in terms of loading and layouts.

When we consider native iOS app development, there is one more reason to go for Sencha Touch. It's the speed of execution in iOS. Sencha Touch is blazing fast on iOS. One can build an app as fast as a native iOS application with Sencha Touch. The Sencha Touch MVC framework is a perfect framework to build and maintain your application. It has a very standard and easy-to-understand flow of development. User interface, business logic, and data access are separate from each other in this architecture, allowing the developer to focus on a particular part without affecting the other part.

So no matter what your preference is, Sencha Touch is an ideal framework to develop mobile applications.

Installation

In this section we will go through the steps for installing Sencha Touch and setting up the environment.

Downloading Sencha Touch

You can download the latest version of Sencha Touch from the Sencha website at `http://www.sencha.com/products/touch/download`. You can download either the commercial or open source version. Both are the same version and free of charge. For this book, we have used the Sencha Touch 2.1.1 GPL version. Download and extract the ZIP file.

Setting up the web server on Mac

Mac OS X has its own Apache web server, or you can install third-party tools such as MAMP. For easy access, we will set up Mac OS X's Apache web server. By default, the Apache web server on Mac OS X is not turned on if you have never used it. To enable it, go to **System Preference | Sharing** and enable **Web Sharing**.

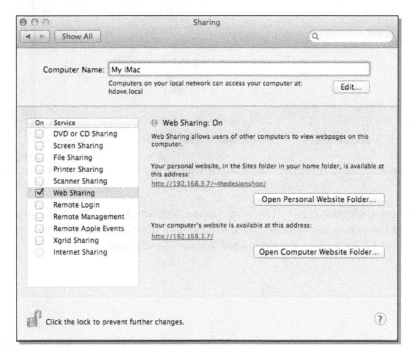

Depending on your Mac OS X setup, it will show the preceding screen. You can click on the respective buttons to go to the website folders, or you can click on the links to check if the sites are working or not. If you see the following screen when you click on the link for the personal website, it means that the Apache web sever is working:

Your website.

Create and publish your own website quickly and easily using iWeb, Pages, and many other applications available for Mac OS X.

It's a snap to create and publish your own website from your Mac. When your site is ready, it's just as easy to publish it.

Open System Preferences and click Sharing, then select Web Sharing.

You're done. Your site is now available on your private network at home or work.

If you're connected to the Internet, your website can also be available to friends everywhere. Just send them the address shown in Sharing preferences.

Apache Power
Web Sharing is built on the Apache web server, an industry standard technology included with Mac OS X. For more information about the Apache web server, see the Apache manual.

Now let's move our Sencha Touch folder into the web server so that we can see it using a browser.

From the **Sharing** window, click on the button **Open Web Site Folder**. Normally, on Mac OS X, this will go to the `Sites` folder. Now create a folder with the name `sencha` and copy all the content from the ZIP file that we downloaded from the Sencha website.

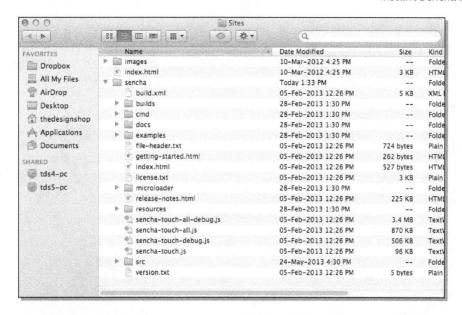

Now open this in a browser with your personal website URL and append `sencha` to it; you will go to examples of Sencha Touch.

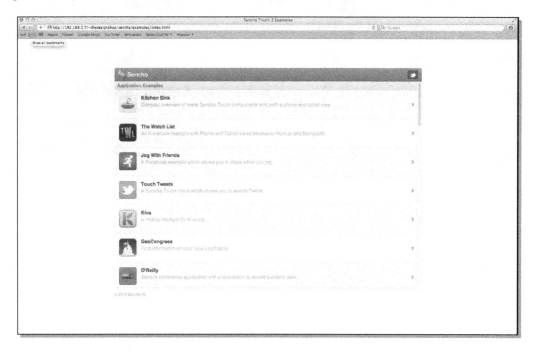

Setting up the web server on Windows

No version of Windows comes with a default Apache server. You may have set up **Internet Information Server** (IIS), but here we are using XAMPP for Windows. You can download and install XAMPP from the following URL: `http://www.apachefriends.org/en/xampp.html`.

After downloading, run the installer.

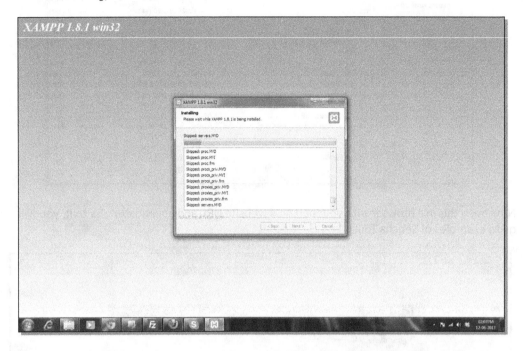

After it's installed, open XAMPP Control Panel and start the Apache web server. There might be issues in starting the Apache server if port 80 is used by other applications. In that case, you might have to stop other applications.

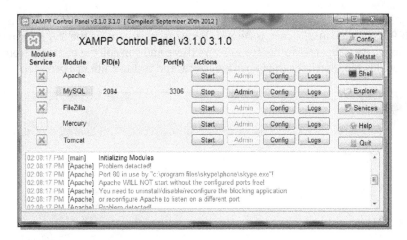

After starting Apache in XAMPP, test it in the browser with either `http://localhost` or `http://127.0.0.1`. If you see the following screen, it indicates that Apache is working:

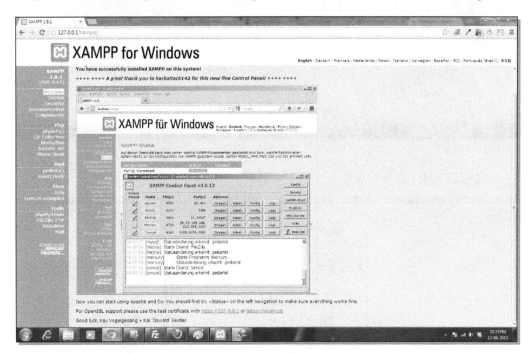

XAMPP is installed in your Windows installation directory. So if you have Windows installed in `C:/`, XAMPP is installed in `C:/xampp`. All XAMPP websites are inside the `C:/xampp/htdocs` directory. So create a separate folder for `sencha` there and copy all the contents from the ZIP file, which we downloaded from the Sencha website, and test the site in a browser.

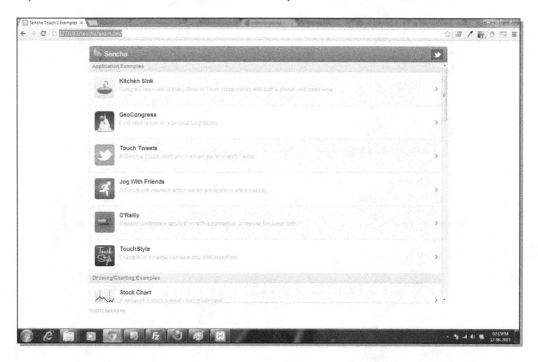

Introduction to Sencha Touch SDK

Once you download and extract Sencha Touch, it will have the following folder structure:

Here, the files for our purpose are `sencha-touch-all-debug.js` and `sencha-touch-all.js`. `sencha-touch-all-debug.js` is the file for debugging purposes, and `sencha-touch-all.js` is a minified version of files for production. You can find CSS files inside the `resources/css` folder. By default, there are five files as follows:

+ `android.css`
+ `apple.css`
+ `bb6.css`
+ `bb10.css`
+ `sencha-touch.css`

Each file can be used for a specific platform. Normally, for development we use `sencha-touch.css`. The `examples` folder contains examples of various classes and components of Sencha Touch. It also contains the **Kitchen Sink** application and many other applications that will give you an overview of Sencha Touch. `src` contains the source code files of Sencha Touch. Here you can see how they organize the framework. We will get back to this in a later section. Sencha Touch also has an online documentation that you can access from the following URL: `http://docs.sencha.com/touch/2.2.1/`.

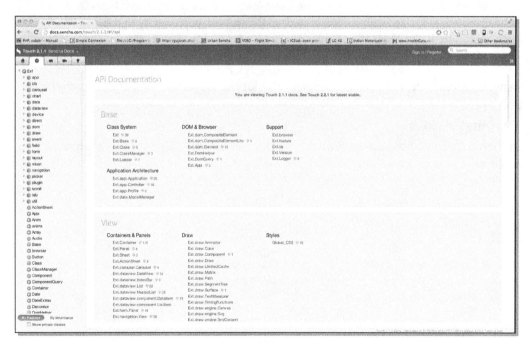

Here you can check the Sencha Touch API with all the classes. This API document is organized according to the class structure, which we will see in a later section. Here you can check a live preview, example code, configs, properties, methods, and events for all the components of Sencha Touch with a small description and examples so that you can use it easily. If you are not sure where to look for, there is an advanced search function here. You can use it to look out for the class or component you are searching. Here you will find some guides and videos about Sencha Touch application development. All the examples are also available here, so you can check it as a reference for your development.

Other folders in Sencha Touch SDK are not too necessary, so we can skip them for now.

Introduction to the Sencha Touch class system

As we know that Sencha Touch is an OOP-based JavaScript framework, it has its own class system. It is well structured to allow OOP-based programming. The whole framework has a global namespace called **Ext**. So each class, components, and methods are covered under this single namespace. Ext itself is a singleton class with some helpful methods. We can directly use it without creating an object of Ext. `Ext.Base` is the base class from which all other classes are inherited. Also, you can inherit any Sencha Touch class and create your own user-defined class. All the other classes follow the same namespace and are grouped inside some other subnamespace in the Ext namespace. Names of the classes map directly to the filepaths in which they are stored. If you check the `src` folder in your Sencha Touch SDK, you will see that they're grouped under folders that follow the namespace. For example, you will find the definition of `Ext.data.Store` inside the `src/data/Store.js` file. This way, all the other classes are defined with suitable namespaces. This way, it's a lot easier to work with Sencha Touch classes.

Defining a class

In Sencha Touch 2, all the classes are defined with the `Ext.define` method while being used in the application. We normally don't use Sencha Touch classes directly (we will see this in later sections). Refer to the following example:

```
Ext.define('MyPanel', {
    extend: 'Ext.Panel'
});
```

The preceding code will define the `MyPanel` class, which extends the `Ext.Panel` class. This is an extended class, so we can add our own methods if needed. All the other members of classes can be defined as key-value pairs.

Defining the configuration of a class

In Sencha Touch 2, the `config` property is introduced to define all the configurations of a class. We can define config properties as key-value pairs. Config properties are totally encapsulated from other class members. In addition to that, an `Ext.class` preprocessor also generates getter and setter functions for each property inside `config`, if there are no getter and setter functions in the base class. Also, it generates the application method for all the `config` properties, which is used internally by setter functions.

```
Ext.define('MyPanel',{
   extend: 'Ext.Panel',
   config: {
      height: 100,
      width: 100
   }
});
```

In the preceding example, we have defined the height and width inside the `config` property. Any other methods are defined outside the `config` property:

```
Ext.define('MyPanel',{
   extend: 'Ext.Panel',
   config: {
      height: 100,
      width: 100
   },
   myFunction: function(){
       //function logic
   }
});
```

Creating an instance of a class

To create a new instance of a class, we use `Ext.create`.

```
var panel = Ext.create('MyPanel');
```

Now we can invoke any member function of the class with the `panel` variable.

Also, we can call functions of the base class, as the user-defined class inherits all the properties and methods of the base class. Additionally, you can override any base class function by adding the function with the same name here in the user-defined class.

```
var panel = Ext.create('MyPanel');
panel.setHtml('My Html');
```

There is also a shorthand way to identify and create components in Sencha Touch with xtype. Each Sencha Touch component has a unique xtype attribute using which we can identify or create an instance of a component. Also, we can define a user-defined xtype attribute. Refer to the following code snippet:

```
Ext.define('MyPanel', {
  extend: 'Ext.Panel',
  xtype: 'mypanel',
  config: {
    height: 100,
    width: 100
  },
  items: [{
    xtype: 'panel',
    html: 'This is Child Panel'
  }]
});
```

In the preceding code, we are adding a child panel item with xtype defined inside the items configuration. Also, we have defined a custom xtype attribute with mypanel. Please note that all the xtype attributes defined in the application should be unique.

Installing Xcode

Xcode is an integrated development environment for developing software and applications for OS X and iOS. This will be needed when we compile our Sencha Touch application to a native application. One advantage of installing Xcode is that it also has simulators for iPhone and iPad, so we can use it to test our Sencha Touch applications in real devices. Xcode is too large to be downloaded, but it can be installed from the App Store in Mac OS X. Open the App Store and search for Xcode.

After installing Xcode, you can use the iPhone or iPad simulator to test the Sencha Touch application from your local Apache server.

Installing Android SDK

You can also download and install Android SDK along with Eclipse. This will be needed to compile and test a Sencha Touch application to the native Android application. You can download Android SDK from the following URL: `http://developer.android.com/sdk/index.html`.

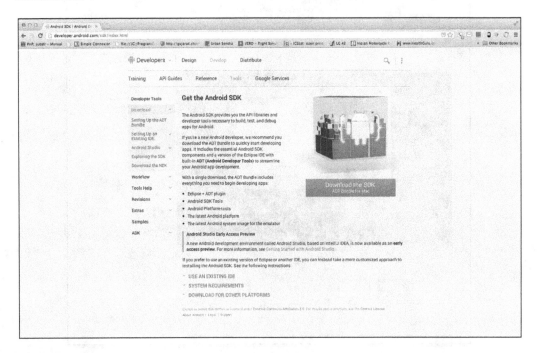

You can also download it from the Eclipse website at `http://www.eclipse.org/`.

After you install Eclipse, you can also install Android Development Tools for Eclipse. Once it's installed, you can have Android device emulators to test Sencha Touch applications on Android devices.

Also, you may want to download Cordova (libraries) for later native application development.

Quick start – building a Hello World application

This section will give more insight on Sencha Touch by introducing some of the controls and components that are widely used in real-time applications.

The Hello World application

In the previous sections, we saw how to set up environments for development of Sencha Touch. Now let's start with the **Hello World** application.

First of all, create a new folder in your web server and name it `sencha-touch-start`. Create a subfolder `lib` inside this folder. In this folder, we will store our Sencha Touch resources. Create two more subfolders inside the `lib` folder and name them `js` and `css` respectively. Copy the `sencha-touch-all.js` file from the SDK, which we had downloaded, to the `lib/js` folder. Copy the `sencha-touch.css` file from SDK to the `lib/css` folder. Now, create a new file in the `sencha-touch-start` folder, name it `index.html`, and add the following code snippet to it:

```html
<!DOCTYPE html>
<html>
    <head>
        <meta charset="utf-8">
        <title>Hello World</title>

        <script src="lib/js/sencha-touch-all.js" type="text/
javascript"></script>
        <link href="lib/css/sencha-touch.css" rel="stylesheet"
type="text/css" />

    </head>
    <body></body>
</html>
```

Now create a new file in the `sencha-touch-start` folder, name it `app.js`, and add the following code snippet to it:

```javascript
Ext.application({
  name: 'Hello World',
    launch: function () {
        var panel = Ext.create('Ext.Panel', {
          fullscreen: true,
            html: 'Welcome to Sencha Touch'
        });
        Ext.Viewport.add(panel);
    }
});
```

Add a link to the `app.js` file in the `index.html` page; we created the following link to `sencha-touch-all.js` and `sencha-touch.css`:

```
<script src="app.js" type="text/javascript"></script>
```

Here in the code, `Ext.application({..})` creates an instance of the `Ext.Application` class and initializes our application. The `name` property defines the name of our application. The `launch` property defines what an application should do when it starts. This property should always be set to a function inside which we will add our code to initialize the application. Here in this function, we are creating a panel with `Ext.create` and adding it to `Ext.Viewport`. `Ext.Viewport` is automatically created and initialized by the Sencha Touch framework. This is like a base container that holds other components of the application.

At this point, your application folder structure should look like this:

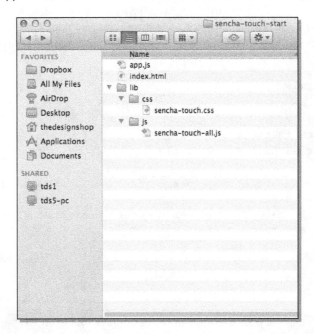

Now run the application in the browser and you should see the following screen:

If your application does not work, please check your web server. It should be turned on, and the steps mentioned earlier should be repeated.

Now we will go through some of the most important features and configurations of Sencha Touch. These are required to build real-time Sencha Touch applications.

Introduction to layouts

Layouts give a developer a number of options to arrange components inside the application. Sencha Touch offers the following four basic layouts:

+ `fit`
+ `hbox`
+ `vbox`
+ `card`

`hbox` and `vbox` layouts arrange items horizontally and vertically, respectively. Let's modify our previous example by adding `hbox` and `vbox` layouts to it. Modify the code in the `launch` function of `app.js` as follows:

```
var panel = Ext.create('Ext.Panel', {
        fullscreen: true,
        layout: 'hbox',
        items: [{
          xtype: 'panel',
          html: 'BOX1',
          flex: 1,
          style: {
              'background-color': 'blue'
            }
        },{
          xtype: 'panel',
          html: 'BOX2',
          flex: 1,
          style: {
              'background-color': 'red'
            }
        },{
          xtype: 'panel',
          html: 'BOX3',
          flex: 1,
          style: {
```

```
                'background-color': 'green'
            }
        }]
    });
    Ext.Viewport.add(panel);
```

In the preceding code snippet, we specified the layout for a panel by setting the `layout:` `'hbox'` property, and added three items to the panel. Another important configuration to note here is `flex`. The `flex` configuration is unique to the `hbox` and `vbox` layouts. It controls how much space the component will take up, proportionally, in the overall layout. Here, we have specified `flex : 1` to all the child containers; that means the height of the main container will be divided equally in a 1:1:1 ratio among all the three containers. For example, if the height of the main container is 150 px, the height of each child container would be 50 px. Here, the height of the main container would be dependent on the browser width. So, it will automatically adjust itself. This is how Sencha Touch adaptive layout works; we will see this in detail in later sections. If you run the preceding code example in your browser, you should see the following screen:

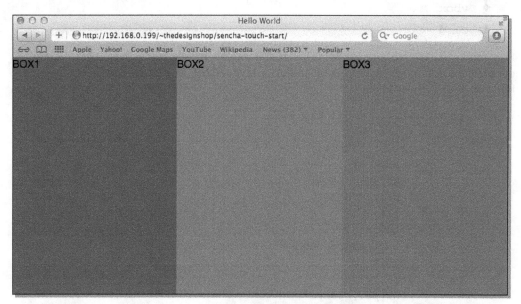

Also, we can change the layout to vbox by setting `layout: 'vbox'`, and you should see the following screen:

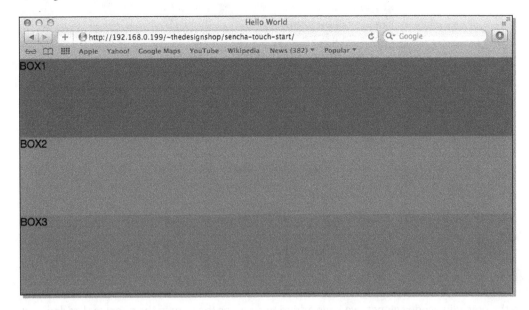

When we specify a fit layout, a single item will automatically expand to cover the whole space of the container. If we add more than one item and specify only the fit layout, only the first item would be visible at a time. The card layout arranges items in a stack of cards and only one item will be visible at a time, but we can switch between items using the `setActiveItem` function. We will see this in detail in a later section.

Panel – a basic container

We have already mentioned the word "panel" in previous examples. It's a basic container component of the Sencha Touch framework. It's basically used to hold items and arrange them in a proper layout by adding the layout configuration. Besides this, it is also used as overlays. Overlays are containers that float over your application. Overlay containers can be positioned relative to some other components. Create another folder in your web server, name it `panel-demo`, and copy all the files and folders from the `sencha-touch-start` folder of the previous example. Modify the title in the `index.html` file.

```
<title>Panel Demo</title>
```

Modify `app.js` as follows:

```
Ext.application({
    name: 'PanelDemo',
    launch: function () {
        var panel = Ext.create('Ext.Panel', {
```

```
                fullscreen: true,
                items: [{
                    xtype: 'button',
                    text: 'Show Overlay',
                    listeners: {
                        tap: function(button){
                            var overlay = Ext.create('Ext.Panel', {
                                                        height: 100,
                                                        width: 300,
                                                        html: 'Panel as
Overlay'
                                                    });
                            overlay.showBy(button);
                        }
                    }
                }]
            });
            Ext.Viewport.add(panel);
        }
    });
```

In the preceding code snippet, we have added `button` as the item in the panel and added listeners for the button. We are binding a `tap` event to a function for the button. On the tap of the button, we are creating another panel as an overlay and showing it using `overlay.showBy(button)`.

The form panel – building rich input forms

The form panel is basically used to create forms such as login forms and registration forms. It's basically used to load and save data. You can add a number of form fields inside the form. Internally, it creates an HTML form. You can submit the form to some URL on your server, get data entered by the user on the server, and save it. Create another folder in your web server, name it `form-panel-demo`, and copy all the files and folders from the `sencha-touch-start` folder of the previous example. Modify the title in the `index.html` file.

```
<title>Form Panel Demo</title>
```

Modify the `app.js` file as follows:

```
Ext.application({
  name: 'FormPanelDemo',
    launch: function () {
        var form = Ext.create('Ext.form.Panel', {
            fullscreen: true,
            items: [{
                xtype: 'textfield',
```

```
                    label: 'Field 1',
                    name: 'field1'
                }, {
                    xtype: 'textfield',
                    label: 'Field 2',
                    name: 'field2'
                }]
            });
            Ext.Viewport.add(form);
        }
    });
```

The preceding code will create a simple form with two text fields. We can also submit the form
to an external user by specifying the **GET** or **POST** method.

```
form.submit({
    url: 'myurl',
    method: 'POST',
    success: function() {
        //logic after submit
    }
});
```

The preceding code snippet will submit the form with the POST method to the specified URL.
Internally, it will create an Ajax request and send all the form fields as POST parameters with
the name mentioned in the form. That's why it's mandatory to apply a name for each field in the
form. Since it's an Ajax request, the `success` property defines a callback function to be invoked
when the form's submission is successful. This is invoked automatically when a response is
received from the server. In the same way, we can have the failure property in case there is some
error in the response or the network is not available. We can retrieve form values by using the
`getValues` function. It will return an object with name-value pairs. For example, refer to the
following code snippet:

```
{
  field1: 'value1',
  field2: 'value2'
}
```

We can set values in the form using the `setValues` function and passing the same object with a
key-value pair. Here, the key should match with the names of the fields in the form. For example,
refer to the following code snippet:

```
form, setValues({
  field1: 'value1',
  field2: 'value2'
});
```

We can group fields inside the form panel using `Ext.form.Fieldset`.

```
{
  xtype: 'fieldset',
  title: 'Fieldset 1',
  instructions: 'Instructions for Fieldset 1',
  items: [{
    xtype: 'textfield',
    label: 'Field 1',
    name: 'field1'
  },{
    xtype: 'textfield',
    label: 'Field 2',
    name: 'field2'
  }]
}
```

Form fields – nifty input fields

We can add a number of fields to the form panel. Sencha Touch has a predefined set of widely used form fields. We can use those fields directly in the form panel by specifying xtype. All the input fields have a clear icon on the right-hand side so that the user can clear the values.

✦ `Ext.field.Checkbox` xtype: `checkboxfield`: This field creates a new version of the HTML checkbox with a nice UI. It is used to select items from a set.

✦ `Ext.field.DatePicker` xtype: `datepickerfield`: This field shows the date picker when tapped. This field is created with the UI close to the native date picker of iOS and Android.

✦ `Ext.field.Email` xtype: `emailfield`: This field creates an HMTL5 e-mail field with a predefined validation for e-mails. When a user leaves the field blank or the value is not proper, it will reset the value.

✦ `Ext.field.Hidden` xtype: `hiddenfield`: This field creates a native hidden field of HTML. It's not visible on the form but it can hold the string or integer value.

✦ `Ext.field.Number` xtype: `numberfield`: This field creates an HMTL5 number field with a predefined validation for the number. When a user leaves the field blank or the value is not proper, it will reset the value. It will also show only the number keypad on mobile devices.

✦ `Ext.field.Password` xtype: `passwordfield`: This field creates an HMTL5 password field. A user can set the characters they want to display for the password.

✦ `Ext.field.Radio` xtype: `radiofield`: This field creates a new version of the HTML radio with a nice UI. It is used to select only one item from a set of items.

✦ `Ext.field.Search` xtype: `searchfield`: This field creates an HMTL5 search input inside the form with a different UI.

- `Ext.field.Select xtype: selectfield`: This is a simple wrapper for the HTML5 select field with a nice UI.

- `Ext.field.Slider xtype: sliderfield`: This field creates a slider with a nice UI and allows a user to select values by sliding the thumb from a range of values.

- `Ext.field.Spinner xtype: spinnerfield`: This field creates a wrapper over the HMTL5 number field with plus and minus buttons so that a user can change the values. A user can specify a min or max value.

- `Ext.field.Text xtype: textfield`: This field creates an HTML text input with a different UI.

- `Ext.field.TextArea xtype: textareafield`: This field creates an HTML text area input with a different UI.

- `Ext.field.Toggle xtype: togglefield`: This field creates a special slider field with only two values and allows the user to select either of them.

- `Ext.field.Url xtype: urlfield`: This field creates a wrapper over the HMTL5 URL field.

The tab panel – a tabbed set of views

The tab panel allows users to switch between various views. Each tab has its own components that will be visible when a tab is tapped. Tabs can be positioned at the top or bottom by using the `tabBarPosition` config. Create another folder in your web server, name it `tab-panel-demo`, and copy all the files and folders from the `sencha-touch-start` folder of the previous example. Modify the title in the `index.html` file.

```
<title>Tab Panel Demo</title>
```

Modify the `app.js` file as follows:

```
Ext.application({
    name: 'TabPanelDemo',
      launch: function () {
          var tabpanel =Ext.create('Ext.TabPanel', {
              fullscreen: true,
              tabBarPosition: 'bottom',
              items: [{
                  title: 'Tab 1',
                  html: 'Tab 1 Content'
              },
              {
                  title: 'Tab 2',
                  html: 'Tab 2 Content'
              }]
          });
```

```
        Ext.Viewport.add(tabpanel);
    }
});
```

We can also show icons for tabs or combine icons with text. Icons can be specified with the `iconCls` config. It accepts a CSS class name here using which we can specify the image to be displayed as the icon.

The navigation view – a smart way of navigation

The navigation view is a new introduction in Sencha Touch 2.0.0. It's much like stack-based navigation. It's basically a container with the card layout, so only one view can be visible at a time. The navigation view defines methods such as `push` and `pop` using which we can control the views. The `push` method is used to add a new view to the navigation view. Normally, we don't use the `pop` method explicitly, as it's used internally by the Back button of the toolbar. The navigation view has the default toolbar docked on top. When we push another view to the navigation view, the back button becomes visible automatically. On the tap of the back button, it will load the previous view. When the first view is displayed again, the back button is hidden again. This all happens internally. The navigation view maintains a stack of views and will load each view based on user action via the `push` or `pop` method. Create another folder in your web server, name it `navigation-view-demo`, and copy all the files and folders from the `sencha-touch-start` folder of the previous example. Modify the title in the `index.html` file.

```
<title>Navigation View Demo</title>
```

Modify the `app.js file` as follows:

```
Ext.application({
    name: 'NavigationViewDemo',
    launch: function () {
        var navigationview = Ext.create('Ext.NavigationView', {
            fullscreen: true,
            items: [{
                title: 'First Item',
                items: [{
                    xtype: 'button',
                    text: 'Push',
                    handler: function() {
                        navigationview.push({
                            title: 'Second Item',
                            html: 'Hello Navigation View'
                        });
                    }
                }]
            }]
        });
```

```
        Ext.Viewport.add(navigationview);
    }
});
```

In the preceding code snippet, we added the navigation view in the viewport with the default item, which is a button. On the tap of the button, we are pushing a new view into the navigation view using `navigationview.push({..})`. This will push a new item to the navigation view. When a new item is pushed, there will be a Back button in the toolbar, and on tapping it, you can go to the previous view again.

Carousels – swipe between views

Carousels allow users to swipe through multiple full-screen views. They will show only one view at a time but allow users to go back and forth with a finger swipe. There are two possible orientations, horizontal and vertical, with carousels. Create another folder in your web server, name it `carousel-demo`, and copy all the files and folders from the `sencha-touch-start` folder of the previous example. Modify the title in the `index.html` file.

```
<title>Carousel Demo</title>
```

Modify the `app.js` file as follows:

```
Ext.application({
    name: 'FormPanelDemo',
        launch: function () {
            var carousel = Ext.create('Ext.Carousel', {
                fullscreen: true,
                items: [
                    {
                        html : 'Item 1'
                    },
                    {
                        html : 'Item 2'
                    },
                    {
                        html : 'Item 3'
                    }
                ]
            });
            Ext.Viewport.add(carousel);
        }
});
```

The preceding code snippet will create a carousel with three items. There are indicators, which show the number of items.

Introduction to data storage

Data package is an important core part of Sencha Touch. It enables the application to persist data through the application using models and proxies. The model defines your business model that is assigned to the store, and the store is used to store a number of records for that store. First, we will define a model.

```
Ext.define('MyModel', {
    extend: 'Ext.data.Model',
    config: {
        fields: [
            {name: field1, type: 'string', defaultValue:'empty'},
            {name: field2, type: 'int'}
        ]
    }
});
```

In the preceding code, we have specified a model with two fields. For each field, we can specify a name, type, and default value. There are various types available, such as `int`, `string`, `number`, `boolean`, `float`, and `auto`. If you are not sure about the type, you can assign `auto`.

Now define a store. Each field in the model can be set when we create an instance of the model using `Ext.create`. Also, you can get or set an individual field using the `get` and `set` functions of the model. For example, refer to the following code snippet:

```
model.get('field1');
model.set('field1','value');
```

Now we will define a store.

```
Ext.define('MyStore', {
    extend: 'Ext.data.Store',
    config: {
        model: 'MyModel',
    }
});
```

In the preceding code snippet, we have defined a store and assigned a model to it. There are a number of ways to load data in the store. We can call the `proxy` method to store and specify a remote `url` value and `reader`.

```
proxy: {
  type: "ajax",
  url : "http://mydomain.com",
  reader: {
    type: "json",
    rootProperty: "root"
  }
}
```

In the preceding code snippet we have specified the `ajax` proxy and the `json` reader. In this case, your remote URL should return a valid JSON output with the root key as `root`. Keys of each object in JSON should match the model fields, only then will they be added to the store, otherwise they are ignored.

Also, we can use the `store.add()` method to add data to the store manually. In the `store` config, we can set `autoLoad: true` to automatically load the store, else use the `store. load()` method.

There are numbers or proxies available in Sencha Touch SDK that we can use, or we can create our own proxy by extending the base proxy class.

List – showing a list of data with custom styles

List is a component that allows you to show data in a list with grouping, indexing, and user-defined format. Create another folder in your web server, name it `list-demo`, and copy all the files and folders from the `sencha-touch-start` folder of the previous example. Modify the title in the `index.html` file.

```
<title>List Demo</title>
```

Modify the `app.js` file as follows:

```
Ext.application({
    name: 'ListDemo',
      launch: function () {
          var list = Ext.create('Ext.List', {
              fullscreen: true,
              itemTpl: '{text}',
              data: [
                  { text: 'Record 1' },
                  { text: 'Record 2' },
                  { text: 'Record 3' },
                  { text: 'Record 4' },
                  { text: 'Record 5' }
              ]
          });
          Ext.Viewport.add(carousel);
      }
  });
```

The preceding code snippet will create a simple list, which will display the records added by the `data` config. `itemTpl` is the config where we can provide a format for the list item. We can also specify the HTML code there. List also works with a store, if we want to display store records in the list. We can assign a store name using the config `store: 'StoreName'`. Any changes in the store will automatically refresh the list.

XTemplate – an advanced template class

The Ext.XTemplate class gives you an advanced templating mechanism with the following features:

+ Conditional processing
+ Autofeeling of an array with the for loop
+ Basic math support

It's normally used with Ext.DataView and Ext.List using the tpl config. Also, it can be used with panels and containers. The following is an example of XTemplate. Create another folder in your web server, name it template-demo, and copy all the files and folders from the sencha-touch-start folder of the previous example. Modify the title in the index.html file.

```
<title>Template Demo</title>
```

Modify the app.js file as follows:

```
Ext.application({
  name: 'ListDemo',
    launch: function () {
        var data = {
            student_name: 'John Mark',
            subjects: [
                { name: 'Maths', marks: '75'},
                { name: 'Science', marks: '60'},
                { name: 'English', marks: '80'}
            ]
        };

        var panel = Ext.create('Ext.Panel', {
            fullscreen: true,
            layout: 'vbox',
            tpl: new Ext.XTemplate(
                    '<p>Name: {student_name}',
                    '<p>Subject ------ Marks ---- Note </p>',
                    '<tpl for="subjects">',
                    '<p>{name} ------ {marks} --- ',
                        '<tpl if="marks &lt; 70">',
                        'Below Average',
                    '</tpl></p>',
                '</tpl></p>'
                )
        });
        Ext.Viewport.add(panel);
```

```
            panel.setData(data);
        }
    });
```

In the preceding code snippet, we have defined a template for the panel and set up data in it. We used the `for` loop to display all the subjects, and the comparison operators to check for marks that are below average and display a note there.

Top 12 features you need to know about

In this section we will see some of the top features of the Sencha Touch framework that you should know in order to build a Sencha Touch application.

Animations

Animations will enhance your application's user interface. They will make it lively. Sencha Touch supports some default animations; you can use them to show your animated views. The following are the animation values supported by Sencha Touch:

- `fade`
- `cube`
- `flip`
- `pop`
- `slide`
- `wipe`

Sencha Touch has the `Ext.Anim` class using which we can run these animations. For example, refer to the following code snippet:

```
Ext.Anim.run(comp, slide, {
    out: false,
    autoClear: true
});
```

In the preceding code snippet, `comp` is the component that we want to animate, and `slide` is the type of animation. We can control animations with some configs.

Also, we can apply animation using the `animateActiveItem` function of the container or panel. For example, refer to the following line of code:

```
panel. animateActiveItem(item,{ type: 'slide', direction: 'right',
duration:2000});
```

The preceding line of code will show the item with `slide` pointing to the `right` direction. We can also control the navigation time with the number of milliseconds in config. Also, animation can be applied to show an overlay.

```
panel.show({ type: 'slide', direction: 'right', duration:2000});
```

The preceding line of code will show the overlay panel with `slide` pointing to the `right` direction. In the same way, we can use other navigation. The `slide` navigation is used by many components such as the navigation view and the nested list. We don't need to specify it.

Adaptive layouts

Sencha Touch's layout engine is quite powerful to make an adaptive layout. It responds to events such as load and orientation change, and adjusts itself quickly. So we don't have to worry about a device's variable width and height; it will automatically adjust itself in any of the devices and in any orientation. We can also bind events such as orientation change, and do manual adjustments if necessary. As we saw in the previous section, we can take advantage of adaptive layout with the `flex` config, and arrange the components horizontally or vertically or create some complex layout. To take the maximum advantage of adaptive layout, we don't assign any height or width to Sencha Touch components unless it's necessary, and it will automatically adjust itself. Any component with the `flex` config will automatically adjust its height and width according to the parent container and relative to other components. The `flex` config can also be mixed with absolute dimensions.

Sencha Touch component queries

A component query is a powerful way to search for components. It can search for components from `Ext.ComponentManager`, a container, a panel, or DOM. There are various ways to find components. If you are looking for a specific type of component, we can use `xtype` to search for the component. For example, refer to the following line of code:

```
container.query('panel');
```

Or:

```
container.query('.panel');
```

The preceding line of code will return all the panels from the specified container in an array. We can search for more than one `xtype` at a time. For example, refer to the following line of code:

```
container.query('panel, gridpanel, tabpanel');
```

In the same way, we can use any `xtype` attribute to search for components. Another way to search for components is with `id` or `itemId`. For example, refer to the following line of code:

```
panel.query('#myitem');
```

It will return all the components that have `id` or `itemId` as `myitem`. While searching with `id` or `itemId`, we have to add # as a prefix, otherwise it will not be able to search. We can also search for components with attributes. For example, refer to the following line of code:

```
container.query('panel[title="MyTitle"]');
```

The preceding line of code will return all the panels from the specified container in an array that has the title `MyTitle`. In the same way, we can also search with other configs and attributes.

We can also find inner components for any particular component. For example, refer to the following lines of code:

```
container.query('#myPanel panel');
container.query('#myPanel > panel');
```

The first line in the preceding code snippet will display all the panels from the component that has the ID myPanel, and the second line of the example code snippet displays only the direct children of the type panel for the component that has the ID myPanel. So the component queries are used to find any components from your application.

Event handling

Most of the Sencha Touch applications are interactive applications. This means that all the components should respond to user events such as touch, swipe, tap, and so on. When an event occurs, we have to take some action. So, it's normally an execution of code when the event occurs. Normally, we execute a function as an action of an event; we call it an event handler. There are two ways in which Sencha Touch can invoke some actions on events as follows:

✦ Event bindings
✦ Controller actions

We will see controller actions in a later section when we will go through the details of the MVC structure. In this section we will see how we can bind events. We should only use event binding when an event and its handler code are available in a single view and do not depend on other views or components in an application. This means that the scope of event handlers is limited to a single view file. So in this case, the declaration of events and events handlers is in a single file, and it cannot be accessed outside that view. So event binding listens to a particular event to be fired and then invokes a function in the same file. The function is called with a certain number of parameters depending on a specific event. For example, create a new folder with the name event-binding0-demo in your local web server and copy all the resources to it as mentioned in the previous section. Create an app.js file and add the following code snippet to it:

```
Ext.application({
    name: 'EventBindingDemo',
        launch: function () {
            var panel = Ext.create('Ext.Panel', {
                fullscreen: true,
                items: [{
                xtype: 'button',
                text: 'Tap Me',
                listeners: {
                    tap: function(button){
                    Ext.Msg.alert('Tap', 'Button Tapped');
                    }
                }
            }
```

```
            }]
        });
        Ext.Viewport.add(panel);
    }
});
```

The preceding code snippet will create a button, and when you tap on it, it will show an alert message. `listeners` is the config for any component to add event handlers. In the preceding code snippet, `tap` is the event and `function` is the handler, which will be invoked when the event is fired. You can add more than one event handler in the `listeners` config for a single component. For example, refer to the following code snippet:

```
listeners: {
    tap: function(){
    },
    painted: function(){
    }
}
```

In the preceding code snippet, we bind two events for a button: `tap` and `painted`. The respective functions will be invoked when the respective events would be fired. In all the cases of event bindings, `listeners` will be invoked in the scope of the parent container. So, the `this` keyword in the respective handler function refers to a component on which the handler method is defined.

Sencha Touch charts

Sencha Touch charts present data to users in various chart formats, and allow users to interact with them through various gestures such as zoom in and zoom out. Built on HTML5, Touch charts will run on any mobile or tablet device. Touch charts also use adaptive layouts to support any width and height of mobile devices, and support both landscape and portrait orientation. Chart legends are also generated based on the available width and height. If there is not much space, legends are displayed as a slide-out menu. In case of enough width, they are displayed inline. We can also configure types of interactions with charts. For example, in a mobile a user can rotate a pie chart, or in a bar chart a user can tap on the bar to view information, or a user can zoom in or zoom out. These interactions are configurable. Touch charts directly work with Sencha Touch's data packages. So you can configure a store for charts and configure a field of charts to be displayed on the respective axes of the chart. You can configure a number of axes and legends for the charts. Chart styling can also be applied with normal SASS styling that we will see in a later section. Let's see a simple example of a chart. Create a new folder `chart-demo` in the web server and copy all the Sencha Touch resources there. Add the following code to the `app.js` file:

```
Ext.application({
    name: 'ChartDemo',
        launch: function () {
```

```
var chart = new Ext.chart.Chart({
    store: {
        fields: ['month', 'revenue'],
        data: [
            { month:'Jan', revenue:100},
            { month:'Feb', revenue:150},
            { month:'Mar', revenue:200},
            { month:'Apr', revenue:50},
            { month:'May', revenue:45},
            { month:'Jun', revenue:100},
            { month:'Jul', revenue:140}
        ]
    },
    axes: [{
        type: 'numeric',
        position: 'left',
        title: {
            text: 'Revenue',
            fontSize: 15
        },
        fields: 'revenue'
    }, {
        type: 'category',
        position: 'bottom',
        title: {
            text: 'Month',
            fontSize: 15
        },
        fields: 'month'
    }],
    series: [{
        type: 'bar',
        xField: 'month',
        yField: 'revenue',
        style: {
            fill: 'blue'
        }
    }]
});
Ext.Viewport.setLayout('fit');
Ext.Viewport.add(chart);
    }
});
```

When you run this code you will see a bar chart. There are two important configurations for any chart: `axes` and `series`. `axes` defines the number of axes, title, and type of axes, and `series` defines the type of chart. We can define more than one series in a single chart. Depending on `series`, the particular configuration is applied. The following are various `series` supported by Touch charts:

+ Area
+ Bar
+ Cartesian
+ Gauge
+ Line
+ Pie
+ Polar
+ Radar
+ Scatter
+ Series

To show a legend for charts, we can add the `legend` config and define its position. Legends are useful when you have more than one series in your chart.

```
legend: {
position: 'bottom'
}
```

Interactions can be added with the `interactions` configs. The following are the types of interactions we can add in charts:

+ ItemInfo
+ PanZoom
+ Rotate
+ CrossZoom
+ ItemHighlight
+ RotatePie3D

All the interactions have a callback function that will be invoked when interaction events are fired with some parameters. For example, refer to the following code snippet:

```
interactions: [{
  type: 'iteminfo',
  listeners: {
    show: function(me, item, panel) {
      panel.setHtml('Revenue is $' + item.record.get('revenue'));
```

```
        }
      }
    }]
```

After adding the preceding `interactions` config, when you tap on any bar of the chart, it will show an overlay panel with some HTML. In the same way, any other interaction can be added to the chart using the callback function. Sencha Touch charts can be rendered only in the fit layout, so make sure that your chart container has the fit layout.

Offline support

As Sencha Touch is built for mobile devices, sometimes it's necessary to have offline support in any application because it might be possible that there isn't any network connection in your mobile device, or there is a special requirement for the application to store data offline. This is like a shopping cart, where we need to preserve items added to the cart till the order is placed. So, it's good to have offline support in your application so that it can run with the network connection once loaded. Sencha Touch supports offline capability with HTML5 local storage. HTML5 local storage is a key-value pair storage, so it will automatically serialize or deserialize data while adding or retrieving data from it. Sencha Touch has the `localstorage` proxy using which we can store data offline. For that, you have to define a store with the `localstorage` proxy. We already saw in the earlier sections that we can either define a proxy with a model or a store. Check out the following example:

```
Ext.define('OfflineModel', {
    extend: 'Ext.data.Model',
    config: {
        fields: ['id', 'name'],
        proxy: {
            type: 'localstorage',
            id  : 'offlineproxy'
        }
    }
});
```

The preceding code snippet will create a model with the `localstorage` proxy and some fields. Here, it's necessary to add a unique ID field in the model, and that will be used as the key while storing data in a local storage. If we don't add it, it will automatically create a field internally. Now let's create a store with the created model.

```
var store = Ext.create('Ext.data.Store', {
    model: 'OfflineModel'
});
```

The preceding code snippet will create a store with an offline model. Now let's see how it works with HMTL5 local storage.

```
store.add({name: 'John Smith'});
store.sync();
```

The preceding code snippet first adds an item in the store and then uses the sync() function. It will add data to HTML5 local storage only when the sync() function is called. So it's necessary to sync the store after any changes. We are not passing an ID, so it will automatically generate a new ID and encode it for local storage. Also, when the application loads or is refreshed, we should use the load() method to load data to the store. The localstorage proxy only works with WebKit browsers, so that could be one disadvantage. Using offline support, our app can work offline and continue storing data offline, and we can build the architecture to synchronize data with the server based on network availability. When you clear the cache of your browser, this data would be removed or you can clear all the data with the localStorage.clear() method.

Fetching remote data with Ajax

Sencha Touch provides users with the Ext.Ajax class to fetch remote data from the server to your applications. Using this class, you can send Ajax requests to the same domain on which your application is hosted. Requests to other domains are blocked. Refer to the following code snippet of a simple Ajax request:

```
Ext.Ajax.request({
    url: 'myUrl',
    method: 'POST',
    params: {
    },
    success: function(response) {

    },
    failure: function(response){

    }
});
```

The preceding code snippet shows a simple Ajax request. success and failure are callback functions. Based on the response of the Ajax request, the respective callback function would be invoked. Data returned from the server is a response object. You can use the Ext.decode function if the server returns JSON data. You can specify the method of the Ajax request and pass any data to the server with the params config, or if you want to send JSON data back to the server, you can use the jsonData config.

The MVC structure

Sencha Touch supports MVC architecture that reduces the development time and improves the application's performance. Also, it's very easy to add new features to the application while using MVC. There are several components of MVC.

Model

Model defines the entities of the application. It manages the data and behavior of the entity. Sencha Touch has a base class, Ext.data.Model, which we can extend to create our own model. We used a model to define some fields or custom fields for entities. For example, refer to the following code snippet:

```
Ext.define('AppName.model.Employee', {
    extend: 'Ext.data.Model',
    config: {
        fields: [
    {
        type: 'int',
        name: 'employee_id'
    },
    {
        type: 'string',
        name: 'employee_name'
    },
    {
        type: 'number',
        name: 'gross_salary'
    },
    {
        type: 'number',
        name: 'allowance'
    },
    {
        type: 'number',
        name: 'net_salary',
        convert: function(value, record){
            return record.get('gross_salary') + record.
get('allowance');
        }
    }
        ]
    }
});
```

This code snippet defines an employee model with some fields. We can define the type and name of the field. Refer to the `net_salary` field, which is a custom field. We have defined the custom function to create a value for it.

View

Views are the UI components of the application. The end user directly interacts with them. All the actions of users are passed to controllers. Views are defined by extending the base Sencha Touch classes. Each view class defines the necessary configs and functions for the view. For example, refer to the following code snippet:

```
Ext.define('AppName.view.MyView', {
    extend: 'Ext.Panel',
    layout: 'fit',
xtype :'customxtype',
    config: {
    flex: 1,
    items: [
        {
            xtype: 'panel',
            items: []
        }
    ]
    }
});
```

This code snippet defines a view by extending the `Ext.Panel` class. It defines all the configs for the panel. We can also define the custom `xtype` attribute for the view that can be used to reference the view in the controller.

Controller

Controller is the most crucial part of the MVC architecture. It defines the event handlers for all the events of the application. It can have references of the views and can show or change the views. All the business logic is written in controllers. Extending the base `Ext.app.Controller` function creates a controller class.

```
Ext.define('AppName.controller.MyController',{
    extend : 'Ext.app.Controller',
    config : {
        refs : {
            customxtype: 'customxtype'
        }
    },
    init : function() {
        this.control({
```

```
        customxtype: {
      }
    });
  }
});
```

This code snippet will create a controller. The `refs` config is used to add references to the views and other components. The `init` function will be invoked when a controller is initialized, and `this.control({ })` is used to add actions for the various events.

Store

Store is used to store and retrieve data from the remote services. Sencha Touch has the `Ext.data.Store` base class, which can be used to extend and create a user-defined class. Store has functions for filtering and sorting. This store binds various data view components such as `Ext.dataview.DataView` or `Ext.List`. For example, refer to the following code snippet:

```
Ext.define('AppName.store.MyStore', {
    extend: 'Ext.data.Store',
    config: {
    autoLoad: true,
        model: 'AppName.model.MyModel',
        storeId: 'myStoreId'
    }
});
```

The preceding code snippet will create a store with a model and other configs.

A sample application

In this section we will build a sample application with the MVC structure. First, we will see how to configure your application for that. We specify all the controllers, models, stores, and views in the application config. First of all, create the `mvc-demo` folder in your web server and copy all the Sencha Touch resources to it. Check out the following steps to start developing a sample application:

1. Create a folder named `mvc-demo`.

2. Create a folder in `mvc-demo` and name it `app`.

3. Create the following four folders inside the `app` folder:

    ○ `model`

    ○ `view`

    ○ `controller`

    ○ `store`

We will build a simple application to manage contacts. This application will first display a list of contacts when it's launched. A user can select a contact to view the details. First of all, create the app.js file and add the following code to it:

```
Ext.application({
  name: 'Contacts',
  models: ['Contact'],`
  stores: ['ContactsStore'],
  views: ['MainView', 'ContactList', 'ContactView'],
  controllers: ['ApplicationController'],
    launch: function () {
        Ext.Viewport.add(Ext.create('Contacts.view.MainView'));
    }
});
```

This code snippet will create the **Contacts** application. Here we have specified the following four new configs in the application.

✦ models

✦ stores

✦ views

✦ controllers

Here we specify the names of all the models, views, stores, and controllers. Ext.Loader will load all the files from the respective folders. Ext.Loader always works with a predefined path. It always assumes that all the models specified here will be available in the app/model folder with the respective filenames. That's why it's very important to give an exact name to files and folders. Now let's create a model. Create a new file with the name Contact.js in the app/model folder and add the following code to it:

```
Ext.define('Contacts.model.Contact', {
    extend: 'Ext.data.Model',
    config: {
        fields: [{
          name: 'id',
          type: 'int'
        }, {
          name: 'name',
          type: 'string'
        }, {
          name: 'email',
          type: 'string'
        }, {
          name: 'phone',
          type: 'string'
```

```
      }],
        idProperty: 'id'
   }
});
```

The preceding code snippet will define a contact model by extending the `Ext.data.Model` class with some fields specified in the `fields` config. Now create a new file with the name `ContactsStore.js` in the `app/store` folder and add the following code to it:

```
Ext.define('Contacts.store.ContactsStore', {
  extend : 'Ext.data.Store',
  config: {
    model: 'Contacts.model.Contact',
    autoLoad:true,
    data: [{
      id: 1,
      name: 'John Smith',
      email: 'john@gmail.com',
      phone: '8503985763'
    },{
      id: 2,
      name: 'Marcus Anthonsen',
      email: 'marcus@gmail.com',
      phone: '2374923874'
    },{
      id: 3,
      name: 'Matt Yang',
      email: 'matt@gmail.com',
      phone: '3473264764'
    },{
      id: 4,
      name: 'Martin  Raymond',
      email: 'martin@gmail.com',
      phone: '3845738457'
    },{
      id: 5,
      name: 'Hung Luu',
      email: 'hung@gmail.com',
      phone: '3483478374'
    }],
    proxy: {
      type: 'memory'
    }
  }
});
```

The preceding code snippet will create a store by extending the `Ext.data.Store` class with some predefined data in the store. Now we will create our main view. Create a new file in the `app/view` folder with the name `MainView.js` and add the following code to it:

```
Ext.define('Contacts.view.MainView', {
    extend : 'Ext.Panel',
    xtype : 'mainview',
    config : {
        layout : 'card',
        items : [{
        xtype: 'contactlistpanel'
    }]
    }
});
```

This code will create a main view of the application by extending the `Ext.Panel` base class. We have added an item in the main view at the start. Note that the `xtype` attribute of this view is specified as `mainview`. It is a user-defined `xtype` attribute. Now let's create a child view. Create a new file named `ContactList.js` in the `app/view` folder and add the following code to it:

```
Ext.define('Contacts.view.ContactList', {
    extend : 'Ext.Panel',
    xtype : 'contactlistpanel',
    config : {
    layout: 'fit',
        fullscreen: true,
        items: [{
            xtype: 'toolbar',
            docked: 'top',
            title: 'Contacts'
    },{
            xtype: 'list',
            itemId: 'contactlist',
            id: 'contactlist',
            itemTpl: '{name}',
            onItemDisclosure: true,
            store: 'ContactsStore'
    }]
    }
});
```

This code will create our list with all the contacts. This view has a toolbar and a list as items. We have used this view's xtype attribute to add it to MainView. This view will display a list of all the contacts with the names. We can change the template the way we want. Now we will display the details of a specific contact that is selected from the list. For this, we have to create a separate view, and we will control that view from the controller. Create a new file with the name ContactView.js in the app/view folder and add the following code to it:

```
Ext.define('Contacts.view.ContactView', {
    extend : 'Ext.Panel',
    xtype : 'contactview',
    config : {
        layout : 'fit',
        items : [{
            xtype: 'toolbar',
            itemId: 'contactViewTopToolbar',
            docked: 'top',
            items: [{
                xtype: 'button',
                ui: 'back',
                text: 'Back',
                itemId: 'btnBackContactView',
                id: 'btnBackContactView'
            }]
        },{
            xtype: 'panel',
            itemId: 'contactpanel',
            id: 'contactpanel',
            tpl: new Ext.XTemplate('<h4>Name : {name}</h4><h4>Email :
{email}</h4><h4>Phone : {phone}</h4>')
        }]
    }
});
```

The preceding code snippet will create a panel with a toolbar and a panel that has a template defined with the tpl config to show the details of the contact. In this code snippet, we have used the ui config with a button. Sencha Touch has some predefined user interfaces for some of the components. The ui config will define the look and feel of the components. Now let's create a controller. Create a new file with the name ApplicationController.js in the app/controller folder and add the following code to it:

```
Ext.define('Contacts.controller.ApplicationController',{
    extend : 'Ext.app.Controller',
    config : {
        refs : {
            mainView: 'mainview',
```

```
                contactListPanel: 'contactlistpanel',
                contactList: '#contactlist',
                contactView: 'contactview',
                btnBackContactView: '#btnBackContactView'
        }
    },
        init : function() {
            this.control({
                contactList: {
                    select: 'onContactSelect'
                },
                btnBackContactView: {
                    tap: 'goBackToContactList'
                }
            });
        },
        onContactSelect: function(list, record){
            if(!this.contact){
                this.contact = Ext.create('Contacts.view.ContactView');
            }
            this.getMainView().animateActiveItem(this.contact, {type: 'slide',
direction: 'left'});
            this.contact.query('#contactpanel')[0].setData(record.data);
        },
        goBackToContactList: function(button) {
            this.getMainView().animateActiveItem(this.getContactListPanel(),
{type: 'slide', direction: 'left'});
        }
});
```

The preceding code snippet will create a controller with the necessary references and event handlers. Please check the `refs` config of the controller. We have added references of our view with the `xtype` attributes and `itemId`. The reference with `xtype` is added with the name of the `xtype` attribute, while the reference with `itemId` is added with the # prefix. This is how we can add a reference to the view or items of the views with `xtype`, `itemId`, or `id` in the controller. Sencha Touch generates a getter function for each reference we have added. For example, to get an active instance of `mainview`, we can use the `getMainView()` function. We can also add a reference with a component query. For example, refer to the following line of code:

```
Panel: '#myPanel panel'
```

This line of code will add a reference of the child panel item of `panel` with the item ID `mypanel`.

The `this.control` section defines the actions or event handlers for the user events. We use the reference we added in the `refs` section to define events and event handlers to it. For example, refer to the following code snippet:

```
contactList: {
select: 'onContactSelect'
}
```

Here we have added a select event, and the event handler is the `onContactSelect` function. Here, `onContactSelect` should be available in the same controller file. This way we can define more than one event and handlers for a single component. Here all the functions execute in the scope of the controller. So this keyword always returns an instance of the controller. So in the preceding code snippet, `onContactSelect` will be invoked with some params when the user selects any record in the list. When a user selects any record, we create a contact view panel if it's not already created, and set the data for the template so that it will display details of the selected contact. The user can go back to the list again by tapping on the back button in this view. `goBackToContactList` is the function executed when the user taps on the back button. Here we have used the `animateActiveItem` function to show the view with animation. So in this way, we can add a number of references to views in controllers and define event handlers for the components in controller files.

Theming in Sencha Touch

In this section we will see how to create a custom theme in Sencha Touch using SASS. Sencha Touch uses SASS to create a new theme.

What is SASS?

Syntactically Awesome Stylesheets (**SASS**) is the CSS preprocessor. It will take a piece of code in a different syntax and convert it to the target syntax. In the case of Sencha Touch, it takes the `.scss` file and converts it into CSS files. So with very less effort, you can generate a CSS. SASS is a Ruby package so you need Ruby to run it. Mac and Linux have Ruby runtime by default, but in Windows you have to install it. On Mac, open the terminal and run the following command:

```
$ sudo gem install sass
```

This will install SASS. Now let's understand a few terms in SASS.

Variables

SASS supports dynamic variables (used to hold some values) that you frequently use in CSS, such as the base color hex value. For Sencha Touch, we have some predefined variables for all the controls that you can find in the API documentation, as shown in the following screenshot:

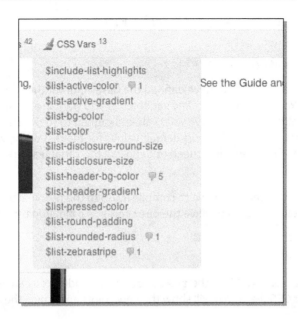

Mixins

They allow users to create re-usable blocks of CSS to be used with the `@include` constructor. Sencha Touch also has predefined mixins for each component that you can find in the API document as shown in the following screenshot:

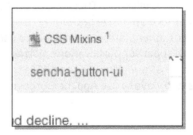

Compass is used to compile the `.scss` file in the case of Sencha Touch. Run the following command in the terminal:

```
sudo gem install compass --pre
```

So to create a custom theme for Sencha Touch, we have to create a new `.scss` file with all the variables declared in it, and then we compile it with Compass; it will generate a CSS for us. You can find the existing `.scss` files in the `resources/sass` folder. Here you can create a new `.scss` file by using variables defined in the API document. The following is an example of a `.scss` file. Save it inside the `resources/sass` folder with the name `custom.sass`.

```
$base-color: #f7f7f7;
```

```
$toolbar-base-color: $base-color !default;
@import 'sencha-touch/default';
@import 'sencha-touch/default/all';
```

In the preceding command lines, we have defined the base color for the whole app and the base color for the toolbar. You can define as many variables as you want in a single `.scss` file, but the variables should be valid and should have valid values assigned to them. The last two statements in the preceding command line will import default values for the rest of the variables, which are not defined here in the file. So we don't need to define all the variables here. Just define what you want to change.

Once the `.scss` file is created, you have to compile it. Go to the terminal and navigate to the `resources/sass` folder where you have the `custom.scss` file. Run the following command in the terminal:

```
Compass compile
```

It will generate a `custom.css` file in the `resources/css` folder. You can attach this CSS file instead of the default CSS file, and it will show the new colors and a new theme.

Native packaging of Sencha Touch applications

When we build an application in Sencha Touch, it is normally a web application, which can run in the browser. Since Sencha Touch works on different platforms, we can wrap a Sencha Touch application using some native wrappers and convert it to a native application. Sencha Touch mimics the look and feel of a native application. There are many native wrappers available for it. For example, Sencha Touch has its own native packaging tool; we can use it to package apps for Android and iOS platforms. For other platforms, we have to use Apache Cordova, formerly known as PhoneGap. Its native wrapper supports various platforms such as Android, iOS, BlackBerry, and Windows. It contains various plugins and APIs to use hardware such as a camera, GPS, and an SD card. There are two ways to use Apache Cordova as follows:

✦ Using PhoneGap Build
✦ Using SDK

Using PhoneGap Build

PhoneGap Build is a Cloud-based build process to build and package apps for various platforms. To build your own applications, upload your Sencha Touch applications on your PhoneGap build account, select the platforms, and trigger the build. In a very short period of time, you get your deployable files. For an iOS build, we need the provisioning profile and developer certificate that we will see in a later section. For this, you have to register at `http://build.phonegap.com`. Once you are signed in, you can create a new application and upload the source files.

Once the source file is uploaded, you can configure application icons, names, version descriptions, and so on.

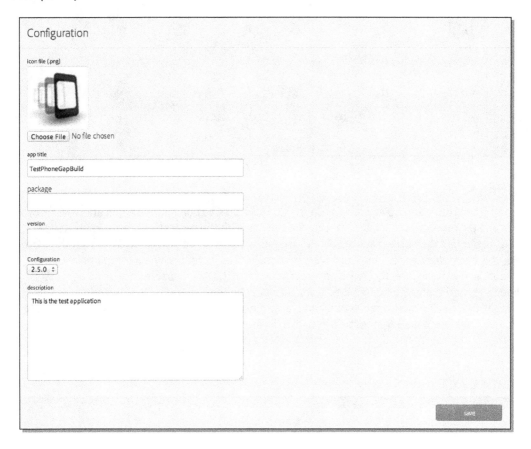

After that, you can trigger the build by selecting various platforms and it will generate the deployable units for each platform.

Using SDK

Apart from PhoneGap build, we can use the Cordova SDK to build native applications. Cordova has an SDK for each single platform that we can use with the respective IDEs such as Xcode or Eclipse to build the native application. For that, first you have to download SDK from the Web. For this example, we are using Cordova 1.5 for the iOS as it creates a new template in your Xcode, and you can directly create an application from it. Other versions are using command-line tools, and that is a bit difficult to start. So select PhoneGap 1.5 from its download site and install SDK for iOS. Now open Xcode and create a new project; you should see a new template named **Cordova-based Application** as shown in the following screenshot:

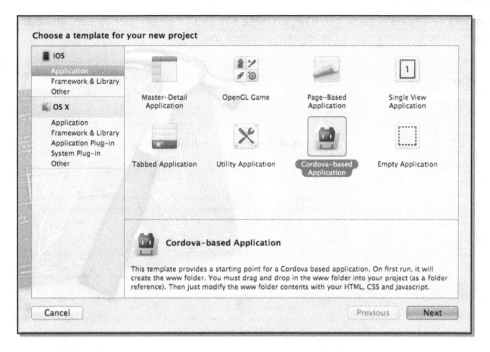

It will create a new project for you. Initially, there is no www folder here. So when you run the application, it will give you an error, but it will generate the www folder inside your app folder. Now right-click on the project in Xcode, click on the **Add Files** option, and add the www folder created inside the project folder. It contains the `Phonegap-1.5.0.js` file and the `index.html` page. `Phonegap-1.5.0.js` is the file that contains all the classes of PhoneGap. It also contains the plugins that are necessary to interact with the hardware and utilize the functionalities for PhoneGap. This file is necessary to include your Sencha Touch's `app.js` file and other files in the `index.html` file. Copy your app folder and other resources here and run the app again; you will see your Sencha Touch application running as a native application. Now the www folder contains all our web assets. This is the starting point for our application. It will also create an icon of the app. Once you run, it will run the application in the simulator. To test it in a real device, you need an Apple developer account and you will have to add the developer certificate and create a provisioning profile. Apple allows you to test the application in 100 test devices. So you also have to register your devices in the Apple developer account. For that, you need the UDID of the device that you can get by connecting your device with the system and check it with iTunes. Once you have registered your devices, create a provisioning profile that will include your developer certificates and device information. You have to use this profile in your device before loading the application in any device. To generate a certificate, you first have to create a certificate-signing request. For this, open a key chain by navigating to **Applications | Utilities**. After that, navigate to **Certificate Assistant | Request a Certificate from Certificate Authority**. It will show you the **Certificate Assistant** window. Enter your name, e-mail address, and choose the option **Save to Disk**. It will save your certificate-signing request to your disk. Now go to your Apple developer account and generate a new certificate by uploading this request.

Once your certificate is ready, you have to create an app ID, register your devices, and generate a provisioning profile. Refer to the following screenshot:

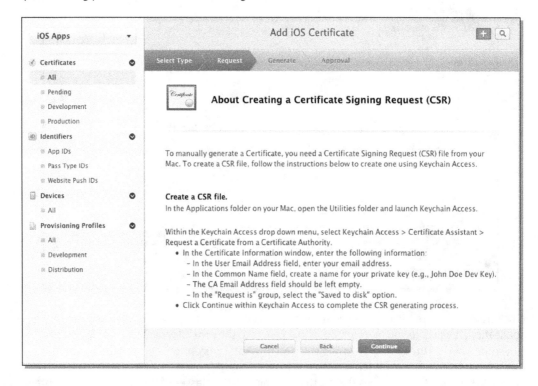

Now download the certificate and the provisioning profile from the account, load it in the device using iTunes, and run the application by connecting the device to your system.

In the same way, we can use this SDK to build projects for other platforms such as Android. For Eclipse, first create an Android application project. Create two new folders in your app, assets/www, and libs folders. Now copy the Cordova JAR files from the SDK you downloaded to the libs folder. Once it's done, we have to configure the build path. For that, right-click on your project and navigate to **Build Path** | **Configure Build Path**. Make sure that the Cordova JAR file is included here, otherwise add it.

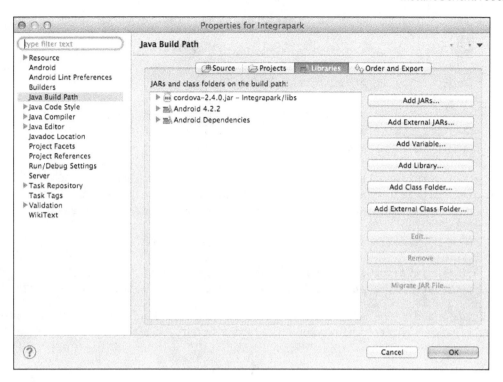

Once it's done, copy the `Cordova.js` file from the SDK to the `assets/www` folder. Now go to your main activity class in the `src` folder and add the following code to it:

```java
import org.apache.cordova.*;

public class MainActivity extends DroidGap {

  @Override
  public void onCreate(Bundle savedInstanceState) {
    super.onCreate(savedInstanceState);
    super.loadUrl("file:///android_asset/www/index.html");
  }
}
```

Also, create an `index.html` file in the `assets/www` folder and add a reference to your Sencha Touch files and resources along with the `Cordova.js` file. Open the `AndroidManifest.xml` file and add the following code before the `<application>` tag:

```xml
<uses-permission android:name="android.permission.VIBRATE" />
<uses-permission android:name="android.permission.ACCESS_COARSE_
LOCATION" />
```

```
<uses-permission android:name="android.permission.ACCESS_FINE_
LOCATION" />
<uses-permission android:name="android.permission.ACCESS_LOCATION_
EXTRA_COMMANDS" />
<uses-permission android:name="android.permission.READ_PHONE_STATE" />
<uses-permission android:name="android.permission.INTERNET" />
<uses-permission android:name="android.permission.RECEIVE_SMS" />
<uses-permission android:name="android.permission.RECORD_AUDIO" />
<uses-permission android:name="android.permission.MODIFY_AUDIO_
SETTINGS" />
<uses-permission android:name="android.permission.READ_CONTACTS" />
<uses-permission android:name="android.permission.WRITE_CONTACTS" />
<uses-permission android:name="android.permission.WRITE_EXTERNAL_
STORAGE" />
<uses-permission android:name="android.permission.ACCESS_NETWORK_
STATE" />
<uses-permission android:name="android.permission.GET_ACCOUNTS" />
<uses-permission android:name="android.permission.BROADCAST_STICKY" />
```

Now compile and run the application and it will run as a native Android application. You can also test this application by connecting your device to your system.

Accessing hardware and native APIs

When we deploy a Sencha Touch application as a native application, we can use some native APIs provided by Sencha to access the hardware of your device. This is one of the major benefits of native packaging of the application. For this, we have a class in Sencha Touch called Ext. device. This class is not actually an API, but it's just a wrapper and can be used to access native APIs provided by Cordova, other third-party solutions, or APIs provided by the Sencha Native packager. As of now, there are four classes in the Ext.device class as follows:

✦ Ext.device.Connection

✦ Ext.device.Notification

✦ Ext.device.Orientation

✦ Ext.device.Camera

Since these native APIs only work when your application is packaged for native deployment, it's not a part of the Sencha Touch build. You have to add them separately using the Ext.require class.

```
Ext.require('Ext.device.Connection');

Ext.application({
    name: 'DemoApplication'
});
```

After that you can use it. For example, refer to the following code snippet:

```
if (Ext.device.Connection.isOnline()) {
    Ext.Msg.alert('Connection Available');
} else {
    Ext.Msg.alert('No Connection Available');
}
```

There are a number of plugins developed for Cordova using which you can access other native APIs that do not exist in the `Ext.device` class. These plugins are composed of a single JavaScript interface for all the platforms and a respective native interface for each single platform. To create your own plugin for Cordova, you have to create a native interface for a particular platform, and create a common JavaScript interface that will be used to invoke native functions.

Thus, in this section, we learned everything we need to know to build real-time applications using Sencha Touch.

People and places you should get to know

In this section, you will see some of the helpful resources that you can use as references while you are developing your Sencha Touch application.

Sencha Touch forum

Sencha maintains an online forum for its products, where community developers can post their questions if they need some clarifications or if they face some issues. You can create an account here and start posting your questions. There are two types of forums:

+ The general forum
+ The premium community forum

The general forum is available for everyone, while to access premium forums you have to register as a premium member. A premium member directly gets support from Sencha product developers and solution engineers. As a premium member, you can request a feature in the next release of Sencha Touch. You can view Sencha Touch's forum at the following URL: `http://www.sencha.com/forum/`.

Here you can see various topics of Sencha Touch. You can search for a topic here. Also, you can report any bugs you may have found while testing the beta release, and Sencha developers will pay attention to it. Many Sencha developers are active on the forum, and they will respond to your queries.

Sencha Touch App Gallery

Sencha Touch App Gallery is the place to show your Sencha Touch application to the world. Here you can submit your Sencha Touch application, and if it's worth showing to the world, they will put your application in the gallery. There are a number of applications already available in the App Gallery in various categories. You can use this App Gallery to see examples of applications for your reference. Sencha Touch App Gallery is available at the following URL: `http://www.sencha.com/apps/`.

Sencha Touch in social media – LinkedIn, Facebook, Google+, Twitter, and Quora

The Sencha Touch community is growing fast on various social networks. There are a number of groups and feeds available on various social networking websites, which you can check for updates.

LinkedIn groups

+ Sencha: `http://www.linkedin.com/groups?gid=2655044&trk=vsrp_groups_res_name&trkInfo=VSRPsearchId%3A4179798313750142712855%2CVSRPtargetId%3A2655044%2CVSRPcmpt%3Aprimary`

✦ Sencha Touch: `http://www.linkedin.com/groups?gid=3167845&trk=vsrp_groups_res_name&trkInfo=VSRPsearchId%3A417979831375014125760%2CVSRPtargetId%3A3167845%2CVSRPcmpt%3Aprimary`

Facebook pages

✦ Sencha Inc. Facebook page: `https://www.facebook.com/senchainc?ref=br_rs`

✦ Sencha Touch developers' community group: `https://www.facebook.com/senchatouch?ref=br_rs`

Google+ page

✦ Sencha Inc. Google+ page: `https://plus.google.com/u/0/+sencha/posts`

Twitter pages

✦ Sencha Inc. Twitter page: `https://twitter.com/Sencha`

✦ Sencha Developer Mitchell Simoens's Twitter page: `https://twitter.com/SenchaMitch`

✦ Sencha Architect Ed Spencer's Twitter page: `https://twitter.com/edspencer`

Quora page

✦ Sencha Touch topic on Quora: `https://www.quora.com/Sencha-Touch`

Sencha Touch blogs

There are a number of developers who write blogs on Sencha. Sencha has its own blogs where you can find updates on various products of Sencha. Sencha's official blog can be found at `http://www.sencha.com/blog/`.

Other blogs related to Sencha are as follows:

✦ `http://miamicoder.com/`

✦ `http://mitchellsimoens.com/`

✦ `http://edspencer.net/`

✦ `http://en.wordpress.com/tag/sencha-touch-2/`

✦ `http://davehiren.blogspot.in`

So, in this section we mentioned various online resources available on Sencha Touch.

Wish you happy coding!

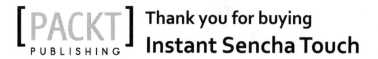

Thank you for buying
Instant Sencha Touch

About Packt Publishing

Packt, pronounced 'packed', published its first book "*Mastering phpMyAdmin for Effective MySQL Management*" in April 2004 and subsequently continued to specialize in publishing highly focused books on specific technologies and solutions.

Our books and publications share the experiences of your fellow IT professionals in adapting and customizing today's systems, applications, and frameworks. Our solution based books give you the knowledge and power to customize the software and technologies you're using to get the job done. Packt books are more specific and less general than the IT books you have seen in the past. Our unique business model allows us to bring you more focused information, giving you more of what you need to know, and less of what you don't.

Packt is a modern, yet unique publishing company, which focuses on producing quality, cutting-edge books for communities of developers, administrators, and newbies alike. For more information, please visit our website: www.packtpub.com.

Writing for Packt

We welcome all inquiries from people who are interested in authoring. Book proposals should be sent to author@packtpub.com. If your book idea is still at an early stage and you would like to discuss it first before writing a formal book proposal, contact us; one of our commissioning editors will get in touch with you.

We're not just looking for published authors; if you have strong technical skills but no writing experience, our experienced editors can help you develop a writing career, or simply get some additional reward for your expertise.

Sencha Architect App Development

ISBN: 978-1-78216-981-9   Paperback: 120 pages

Develop your own Ext JS and Sencha Touch application using Sencha Architect

1. Use Sencha Architect's features to improve productivity

2. Create your own application in Ext JS and Sencha Touch

3. Simulate, build, package, and deploy your application using Sencha Command and Sencha Architect

Sencha Touch 2 Mobile JavaScript Framework

ISBN: 978-1-78216-074-8   Paperback: 348 pages

Get started with Sencha Touch and build awesome, native quality mobile web applications

1. Learn to develop web applications that look and feel native on Apple iOS, Google Android, BlackBerry 10, and Windows Mobile devices using simple examples

2. Design and control the look of your application using a variety of simple style settings and themes

3. Make your application respond to the user's touch with events such as tap, double tap, swipe, tap and hold, pinch, and rotate

Please check **www.PacktPub.com** for information on our titles

PhoneGap 2.x Mobile Application Development Hotshot

ISBN: 978-1-84951-940-3   Paperback: 388 pages

Creating exciting apps for mobile devices using PhoneGap

1. Ten apps included to help you get started on your very own exciting mobile app

2. These apps include working with localization, social networks, geolocation, as well as the camera, audio, video, plugins, and more

3. Apps cover the spectrum from productivity apps, educational apps, all the way to entertainment and games

Sencha MVC Architecture

ISBN: 978-1-84951-888-8   Paperback: 126 pages

A practical guide for designers and developers to create scalable enterprise-class web applications in ExtJS and Sencha Touch using the Sencha MVC architecture

1. Map the general MVC architecture concept to the classes in ExtJS 4.x and Sencha Touch

2. Create a practical application in ExtJS as well as Sencha Touch using various Sencha MVC Architecture concepts and classes

3. Dive deep into the building blocks of the Sencha MVC Architecture including the class system, loader, controller, and application

Please check **www.PacktPub.com** for information on our titles

* 9 7 8 1 7 8 2 1 6 5 9 8 9 *